STORIES IN THE STARS

THE STORY OF PERSEUS

By Blanche Roesser

Gareth Stevens
PUBLISHING

leveled reader

Please visit our website, www.garethstevens.com. For a free color catalog of all our high-quality books, call toll free 1-800-542-2595 or fax 1-877-542-2596.

Library of Congress Cataloging-in-Publication Data

Roesser, Blanche, author.
 The story of Perseus / Blanche Roesser.
     pages cm. — (Stories in the stars)
 Includes bibliographical references and index.
 ISBN 978-1-4824-2681-6 (pbk.)
 ISBN 978-1-4824-2682-3 (6 pack)
 ISBN 978-1-4824-2683-0 (library binding)
 1. Perseus (Greek mythology)—Juvenile literature. 2. Constellations—Folklore—Juvenile literature. 3. Mythology, Greek—Juvenile literature. I. Title.
 BL820.P5R64 2016
 292.1'3 |2 23
                                            2015007003

Published in 2016 by
Gareth Stevens Publishing
111 East 14th Street, Suite 349
New York, NY 10003

Designer: Samantha DeMartin
Editor: Therese Shea

Photo credits: Cover, pp. 1, 19 Luciano Corbella/Getty Images; p. 5 Yganko/Shutterstock.com; p. 7 PHAS/Universal Images Group/Getty Images; p. 9 Dogstock/Shutterstock.com; p. 11 DEA PICTURE LIBRARY/De Agostini Picture Library/Getty Images; p. 13 piotrwzk/Shutterstock.com; p. 15 Guillaume Piolle/Wikimedia Commons; p. 17 DIRECTMEDIA/Wikimedia Commons; p. 21 European Southern Observatory/Wikimedia Commons.

Printed in the United States of America

CPSIA compliance information: Batch #CS15GS: For further information contact Gareth Stevens, New York, New York at 1-800-542-2595.

CONTENTS

Hero in the Stars .4

Meet Perseus .6

Medusa 12

Andromeda 16

A Shower of Meteors 20

Glossary .22

For More Information 23

Index 24

Boldface words appear in the glossary.

Hero in the Stars

A constellation is a group of stars that forms a shape. Constellations are named for their shapes. The constellation called Perseus is named for a hero from Greek **myths**. Do you think the stars look like a person when they're connected?

5

Meet Perseus

Stories about Perseus begin with a king named Acrisius (uh-KREE-see-uhs). An **oracle** told the king that he would be killed by his grandson. So, Acrisius hid his daughter Danaë (DAA-nuh-ee) to keep her from having children.

Danaë

7

However, Zeus (ZOOS), the king of the gods, fell in love with Danaë. Soon, she had a baby boy she named Perseus. When her father found out, he put them both in a wooden chest and threw it into the sea.

Zeus

9

Zeus made sure the chest floated safely to an island. A fisherman named Dictys (DIHK-tihs) found the mother and son. They stayed with him as Perseus grew up. However, Dictys's evil brother was the king of the island.

Medusa

King Polydectes (pah-lee-DEHK-teez) wanted to marry Danaë. Perseus guarded his mother from the evil king. So, Polydectes commanded Perseus to bring him the head of the monster Medusa. All who looked at her turned to stone. However, the gods helped Perseus.

Medusa

13

The gods gave Perseus **sandals** to make him fly. He got a helmet that made him **invisible**. He received a **shield** he used to see Medusa without being turned to stone. Perseus cut off Medusa's head and put it in a bag.

15

Andromeda

While flying home, Perseus saw a princess named Andromeda below. She was chained to a rock. He saved her from a terrible sea monster. Next, Perseus went home. He took Medusa's head to Polydectes. When Polydectes saw it, he turned to stone.

17

Perseus and Andromeda were married. At their wedding, Perseus used Medusa's head to turn Andromeda's evil uncle to stone. A constellation is named for Andromeda, too. Both constellations are near each other in the night sky.

19

A Shower of Meteors

Every summer, people can see a special **meteor shower**. It's called the Perseid meteor shower, because it begins in the Perseus constellation. Many meteors burn brightly as they move in the night sky. Look for it from mid-July to late August!

GLOSSARY

invisible: unable to be seen

meteor shower: an event in which a number of meteors, made of space rock or metal, can be seen moving from one point in the night sky

myth: a story that was told by an ancient people to explain something

oracle: in ancient Greece, a person through whom a god was believed to speak

sandal: a light, open shoe with straps worn during warm weather

shield: a large piece of metal, wood, or other matter carried for protection

FOR MORE INFORMATION

BOOKS

Chen, P. K. *A Constellation Album: Stars and Mythology of the Night Sky.* Cambridge, MA: New Track Media, 2007.

Harkins, Susan Sales. *Perseus.* Hockessin, DE: Mitchell Lane Publishers, 2008.

Hoena, B. A. *Perseus and Medusa.* North Mankato, MN: Stone Arch Books, 2014.

WEBSITES

Perseus
www.historyforkids.org/learn/greeks/religion/myths/perseus.htm
Find out more about the adventures of Perseus.

Perseus Constellation
www.constellation-guide.com/constellation-list/perseus-constellation/
Read about the stars of the Perseus constellation.

INDEX

Acrisius 6

Andromeda 16, 18

Danaë 6, 8, 12

Dictys 10

gods 8, 12, 14

helmet 14

hero 4

Medusa 12, 14, 16, 18

meteors 20

myths 4

oracle 6

Perseid meteor
       shower 20

Polydectes 12, 16

sandals 14

sea monster 16

shield 14

wooden chest 8, 10

Zeus 8, 10